Obstacles of Love

Author Eugenia James

Cover by Eugenia James

Illustrated by Eugenia James

Edited by Eugenia James

ISBN:9798307191460

Printed In United States

Published by Eugenia James

Table of Content

Chapter 1

Family

Can You Focus On Me

Can you focus on me and only me

Can you be the man I need you to be

Can you be faithful even when I'm not around

Can you treat me as the most valuable diamond found

Can you be my strength on my weak days

Can you hold me if I leave and want me to stay

Can you have my back with the world on my shoulders

Can you be my warmth if my heart gets colder

Can you make me feel like my dream has come true

Can you be the man that I see in you

Can you see me as perfect, as well as not

Can you love me from my soul, because my soul is all I got

~U GenUis~

Is It You

The ways I desire you is almost embarrassing to me

Due to I've never been so connected to someone, completely

It's not about nothing you have, but your vibe and smile

It's something about your persona…I don't care about your lifestyle

I just want to keep you around for awhile

Friends are what we are

Yet you are the star

That attracts my eye

However I'm still afraid to try

To allow myself to not be scared with you and yes I know why

It's simply because you make my Spirit smile with easier

I just pray daily that this is no tease

Understand my fears and why they're there, please

~U GenUis~

When You Came Back

Everything about you is imperfectly perfect to me

From the strength in your voice to the sparkle in your eyes that lights only for me

You're smile is gentle…it brightens my darkest days and to never lose you again in what I often pray

Could it be the comforting words that lets me know I'm felt, not just heard…or the knowing that I am not just another curse word

Every effort you put forth in making me smile is definitely noticed, it's been awhile

It's a significant feeling I desire that I haven't had since I had you…not sexual, not physical, it's like my spirit needs you

Leave me thinking that love at first sight is really real…it just took my heart to heal to ACCEPT love…allowing myself to accept and feel what's real

I admit I'm afraid to be happy because happiness can be taken but you're more of a blessing to me, that's no faking

God knew I needed you as you needed me…He has shown me favor by bringing you back to me…

~U GenUis~

Don't Mislead Me

Don't tell me, "I got you" when you know that you don't

It's not because you can't, it's because you just simply won't

Won't even try to excuse yourself

To see where I need help

But yet, when I'm mad

You try to justify yourself and the hard times you're having or had

Not seeing that I put me to the side to be your comfort

But when I'm weak, your strength is something I yearn for

Yet I get this nonchalant, arrogance that pushes me so far

It mutes me

Makes me feel like you are playing with my dignity

Now here goes none of me

I don't call, nor text to control my mentality

Or feeling like you have used and manipulated me

Feeling like you tampered with my integrity

But see if it wasn't for God having mercy on you and Grace on me

I would have been on some gutter shit...you tried to fuck with my energy

But aht aht...

You must forgot

About the shine I got

You already know I'm too cold to be hot

Fake on me...NOT

Leaving your mind open like dot...dot...dot...

~U GenUis~

Don't...

Don't fuck me like you love me if you don't want that mindset

Don't fuck me with your feelings, you can't handle that yet

Don't fuck me with emotions when you don't own none

Don't fuck me like you need me when you gone eventually be gone

Don't fuck me like you value me knowing to you, I'm valueless

Don't fuck me and ignore me like you could care less

Don't fuck me in my bed, accepting good head

Don't fuck me unprotected knowing you were a "thin" thread

~U GenUis~

Unexplained Connection

Ever met something so real

That you didn't know how to feel

It's new but true

Its something I'm trying to explain to you

Ever saw pain yet hurt in someone's eyes

That gave you drive you can't disguise

Mentally thinking if that person is a prize

Yet collecting yourself

Praying things don't go left

Acknowledging this person makes you believe that someone can love you out there

They give you the energy you've desired, fast for and prayed

But yet you're afraid

Afraid due to fear of pain

Scared to release and be free with your heart, wondering if it's insane

To find exactly what you needed in one woman…but in my case, ONE MAN!

~U GenUis~

Butterflies

If butterflies was a person I'll fly into your arms

The strength in your voice, make my heart warm

Thinking of you makes my soul smile

And must I say…it's been awhile

Awhile since I've made a glow in a man's eye

A feeling that turns me on…wonder why ?

You see me as a person before a playmate

This feeling is beyond GREAT

YOU make me weakened but yet STRONG

If what I'm feeling is right, I'm ok with being wrong

I don't care what it looks like or what the people say

What's mines is mines, but you know that anyway

Your smile is so giving life with strength inclined

I lay in my bed a pray that God sent you to be mines

~U GenUis~

Black Man, Black Man

Will you allow me to give you a hand

Be your ear to understand

Without judgment of who you are as a Black Man

Can I support your spine

When you feel your feel frame isn't aligned

Be your mental release

Allow me to learn to be your peace

Can you allow my shoulder to be your pillow

My shirt to be your tissue when your soul feels low

Just like the clavicle, as we say collarbone

Allow me to support you, no matter if you're right or wrong

Listen Black Man, as I feel your heartbeat

Allow me to rub your back and release the heat

From having to defeat

The daily diversities of these city streets

Black Man, allow me to humble your heart but strengthen your mind

Be your bifocals, although you're not blind

Be your soul desire when you want to unwind

Understand Black Man that your worthiness is beyond mankind

Listen Black Man, I'm focused on you

See we need Kings like you to lead our youth

We need you Black Man, this is our undeniable truths

Stand...STAND UP with your hair, nails and every tooth

DEAR BLACK MAN...THE ONE RIGHT HERE...I'M ROOTING FOR YOU

~U GenUis~

Heartbreak

When will it be OK for me

To openly

Express my needs...my desires genuinely

Can I trust you to listen when I want to be heard

Like can I trust your words

If needed can me and you, together, go against the world

Can I...just can I...be vulnerable

I mean is that even tolerable

Tolerable with you...Or will you treat me dishonorable

Can I trust you to hold me

Console me

When I can't explain my energy

I'm asking you, baby, to please…please baby just listen to me

What happens if my health took a bad turn

I need for you to stand stern

When I feel low

I need you to be the light that makes me glow

I mean I need you to enhance me, you know

I need you to not only be my mate, but be my everything

And no, I'm in no rush to get a ring

However, understanding that I need you to do manly things

Bring the masculinity

Yes...I admit I desire that kind of energy

I want to feel appreciated

Not designated

To be the woman I am without hesitation

But remember, I can't be Her without appreciation

I need you to protect my heart as if it belonged to your mother

I need you to pray for my soul...shall I go any further

If I gave you

Like gave you instructions to my heart, what would you do

Would you aim to protect it like yours

Or take me on a heartbreaking tour

~U GenUis~

Fuck Love

I once thought that love was the place for me

But see that's too rich for my blood, it hurts endlessly

It looks and feels so good in the beginning

However in my world, it always ended

Yes, I know how to love but don't seem to get that shit it back

Just like building a train with no wheels to track

Love...FUCK YOU

I thought you were true

I believed in you

How do you let lust be a blinding concept of you

Lust share your feelings and similar emotions

Like seeing a pond but expecting an ocean

You allow lust to even wear your damn skin

And expect us to know the difference when yall are looking like twins

Although lust seems to outweigh love, at what point do we try love again

However, They say real love is what lasts until the end

~U GenUis~

Surreal Love

While what I thought was real

Your heart was made of steel

The way you made me feel was unreal

I should have known WE wasn't apart of your deal

Shit just went left field

So now I'm sitting and thinking…I feel used

My genuine heart was abused

I'm so confused

I feel my heart have been bruised

What lasted for only weeks

Seems to have me weak

I let my guards down and even became your biggest freak

I prayed for your strength

My humbleness is what I resent

Wishing I never went to such measurements

To show you what realness really meant

I feel broken on the inside

But these feelings I have to hide

Holding on to my pride

Trying to walk straight with shattered piece because I will not lose my stride

Find me

Lost,

Searching to be loved but not at a

mental cost

Mentally, I cannot afford to lose the person that I've become, trying to be good for you

I need for you to accept me for my genuine heart and honest truths

I'm lost, searching to feel

To feel a feeling that mentally heals

The emotional part of me that makes it hard to deal

Or even maybe the part that don't acknowledge what's real

I need your Spirit to be one the equally heals

I'm in search of someone to open their hearts to share

The share the space within, even if there's limited space there

Just care

Care enough to not leave me in despair

In return, I will always push to be your breath of fresh air

To protect you as I want you to protect me

To love you as I desire…very deeply

Intimately

Spiritually

Genuinely

So I'm on my best behavior, awaiting for you to find me

~U GenUis~

Perfect Imperfection

Just the sound of the phone when your text message rings

Plays a melody in my heart that I have yet to sing

But when that phone rings and I see that it's you

I feel like back in high school when love was pure, innocent and felt true

Being mesmerized with just mere thoughts of life with you

But yet, back to reality, asking myself, is this true

The feeling of wanting to be in your presence

The profound feeling of protection

That gives me comfort to open up my affection

Security in knowing that my heart have made the right connection

To feel free but yet loved is the best form of imperfect perfection

~U GenUis~

But Real Tho???

Thoughts in my mind consume my happiness due to thinking things could be better than what they are.

Thinking that I would one day find love that loves me back...wondering if this is my life, the happiest it gets.

Hearing people say, "there's someone for everyone"...I really believed that shit.

Until I can only get past a couple of months before I let go due to realizing the strength that I've shown was way too much to show.

Either a strong man that sees absolutely no personal interest in you or a broke man that shows all interest in you..

There seems to be no in between, where the two meet in the middle. Like a man that is strong but yet shows all interest in me...leaving me without a question to ask or a worry to have.

I'm so over trying to be with someone...my mental me is not ready.

I mean, as we are all grown, I shouldn't even have to tell a man how to treat me...

~U GenUis~

Waiting On Him

I don't like heartache…but I don't fuck with pain

Yet I desire to love, yeah, I know that shit sounds insane

Like poisonous venom to the membrane

Seeing the very best in others, but always seems to fail

Failing at this shit called love…or is it just a fairy tale

It seems like a bad dream or did I bump my head on a rail

When I be receiving the energy of betrayal

Leaving me waiting to exhale

But STOP!…first I must inhale

Relax and breathe to stay out of this steel shell

One that makes me misinterpret what could be

If only I release this bad energy

From past pains and tormented agony

From needing a little strength but no one stood for me

Causing me to go into a mental state of being lonely

Only to find out that you nor you could ever love me…

Like I love me

Yet I desire the core of love…love is in my true destiny

Learning patience along the way because to encounter real love…I'll await patiently

Endlessly

But I will receive it..TRUE LOVE…INDEFINITELY

~U GenUis~

Pour Into Me

Don't want me, desire me

Don't tolerate me, admire me

Don't scold me

Just hold me

Console me

But please don't try to control me

Dont leave me

Nor mislead me

But lead me

Allow me to enhance my femininity

Don't judge my pains

That shit is insane

Don't rain on me

Don't drain from me

Comfort me

Restore my energy

Protect me from silent enemies

Search for the best part of me

My soul...my spirituality

See the genuinity

That makes me admirably

ME...

That's right...just me

~U GenUis~

Steel Love

Back to the butterflies and smiles that I once known

Along with the feeling of love that's been unknown

Being able to share pains

That's been driving me insane

While trying to hold it all in have been an inevitable pain

Back to feeling secure in knowing I'm cared for

Is a feeling I've also prayed for

A desiring need, I can't ignore

Just like every bedroom needs a door

Because of being my own backbone

Have made me grow so strong

So strong that I have honestly been alone

Yet, this is old but still new

Somehow I have high hopes of me and you

I just ask that you don't change like these lames

Like take my heart and play games

Just love me as I love you

Then there is nothing in this world that we can't get through

~U GenUis~

Cost Of Love

Love is free…love is taught

Real, true love can't be bought

Love loves unselfishly

Although sometimes love seems to hurt you and me

Love sees pain without speaking a word

Revealing the unspoken so that it's heard

Love, oh love why do you sometimes hurt so bad

Love…why do you sometimes leave me sad

Love…can you feel my pains

Love oh Love protect me and keep me sane

~U GenUis~

Stress Relief

Smiling a smile that I've longed for

Loosening the fear of people walking out of the door

To never be seen anymore

You came into my life when I was a mess

There is no reason for me to feel none other than blessed

Feeling your touch releases my stress

Calming a feeling of tension in my chest

It's been times that I've wondered where did you come from

However I believe in God for more blessings to come

Thank you for allowing me to succumb

The lost feeling of being alone

Thank you for not giving up on me

The person you met was crushed indefinitely

But you…your touch…your SPIRIT filled me genuinely

~U GenUis~

Fight For You

If loving you is wrong, I'm ok with not being right

If I had to fight for your heart, that'll be my most courageous fight

If it leads to being your peace at night

Your joy even when I'm not in sight

Knowing that together, we'll forever be aight

Nights without you

Seems to be the darkest shades of grey and blue

Longing to be back in the presence of you

Let's start with your smile and how it glows

Even Ray Charles's eyes can see your happiness show

We share a love from years ago

A love that waited, although times got hard

Sometimes got harder than gambling with marked cards

Yet, you never gave up…you would always come back

Expressed feeling that some may think seems wack

In my eyes, you became a stronger man and these are facts

~U GenUis~

Ready To Love

Come here and let me love you

I want to touch you

Feel you

Mold you

Be consoled by you

Let me feel your pains

Make dry of your rain

I don't want to refrain

From the woman I am again

Can I be gentle

Gentle with you and you protect my mental

While you put me back to pieces and remold me as your medal

Allow me to treat you like a man

Because with strength you stand

Fighting the world back to back as I am always your best hand

So come on here and let me caress you and rub on that back

We both know that you're in desiring need of that

Allow me to pull all the stress out of your body

Yes the entirety

Feeling your flesh and every thumping heartbeat

Which is why you always win when you bet on me

~U GenUis~

Sleepless Nights

Sleepless nights

My mind is on an ongoing flight

Got me wondering is what I'm feeling even right

Is it right…well let me say ok

Ok for me to be thinking…or even feeling this way

Am I becoming too vulnerable because I like your presence

Because I admire your essence

Yet the thought of verbally expressing these emotions have my throat feeling all tense

Like being the only one left sitting on the bench

Hard swallowing

Because everything in me is hollering

"I desire your touch"

But wait…maybe I'm doing too much

This feeling is giving me an emotional rush

When I see your face, I try to hide my blush

Damn damn damn…I can't let this be known

I have to hover these feelings like a damn drone

Secretly thinking if wanting you ain't right, I don't mind being wrong

Just as long as at this moment, this is where I belong

It's hard to sleep, with thoughts of you on my mind

I never imagined that our vibe would be one of a kind

I fought long enough to act blind

Got my emotions and masculinity in a bind

Emotions say be soft...its ok

To be nothing but a lady

But my masculinity

Gets the best of me but can be calmed by the man with mental stability

Which is why it's you

Yes you

Your energy, your vibe and the motivation I receive from you

Is everything I desire but with patience, I'll wait for you

~U GenUis~

Humbling Energy

How do I express

Express this feeling of gentleness

That derives from the tenderness

That's felt within my soul with every single stroke of your fingertips…even your toughness

The strength of you pulls the masculinity from me

The tension from the stress of the hard days I see

Your smile is becoming a healing place for me to find peace…emotional sanity

Yet, your eyes have become a magnifying glass for me

To see that humbleness comes from an emotional connection a stronger energy

Seeing my happiness and brighter days through your eyes

Shines like a star through cloudy skies

In return

I yearn

To apply first aid nursing to your every burn

Even be there for the healing process

That normally causes stress

Because it can sometimes be a mess

However, I feel your heart as you have allowed mines to happily rest

Rest in knowing what's real is real…this is no test

~U GenUis

True Chemistry

I love it when you grab me

Squeeze me

Hold me tight

It feels good when you're smiling,

Not frowning

And everything is alright…

When I know you have a desiring need for me

Because this love thing we share is easy to see

Your eyes glow even from a distant sight of me

Which is why my desire is to enhance this energy

Of love and heartfelt ecstasy

Because true chemistry

Is the blessing I've awaited for patiently

To be genuinely

Yet uniquely

Yoked equally

If this was checkers…just King me

Yes sir, my heart has been captured, indefinitely

~U GenUis~

Feeling Your Vibrations

Lost without you

While being found within you

Inhaling the scent of your skin

Envisioning the spread of you jawline when you grin

Feeling the Spirit that your vibe releases from within

Ohhh how is it such

That I yearn for the sound of your voice so much

Why…just why does my body tingle at the thought of your touch

Why do my heart flutter when I see that your car pulls up

Tell me just how do your ears not burn

Just like the wheels on the rollercoaster…you make my mind turn

I can see your smile even when you're not around

It's like your heartbeat has become my favorite sound

~U GenUis~

Desiring You

Catching my thoughts including you, just the simple things

Like the way your eyes shine just at the sight of my being

The way your eyes follow me from way across the room

Just like when the warm rays of sun shines and the roses bloom

Finding myself studying you

Not intentionally

However, it just amazes me to see within the man you present visually

That pain you hold mentally

The strains that holds you emotionally

Yet, you see me, genuinely

I'm thinking...I'm wondering how to appreciate you wholeheartedly

How to make your smile greater

As you do for me, rather now or later

I'm in woe with every conversation

It shows Spiritual determination

Also your strength to overcome any situation

Gives me inspiration

Inspiration in knowing that it's ok to smile without hesitation

You got me feeling all free

Free to genuinely, just be me

That goofy, yet loud girl that hmmm wants to just be...

Just to be desired...desired wholeheartedly

~U GenUis~

He's In My Mind

I was trying to to be clean

But it's this man that has all of what it takes to make me not be mean

He caress my body and ease my mind

Takes the pressure from my body with every hotspot he finds

Ooouuuu this man…this man

The strength that he has when he walks on land

Ummm with every stroke of his fingers

I feel electricity through my body like when I hear good singer

He holds me….

Damn…he holds me so securely

In the peak of his sleep, this man holds me

Head on his chest, yet he can feel my heartbeat

Beating rapidly

All because of this energy that I have long desired is laying right next to me

In my mind, I'm thinking this has to be a fantasy

Shit…If only y'all could feel what I feel

When I'm climbing his hill

Working my every skill

Enhanced by his strength and yet my energy kills

When I can climb no more and my body gets weak, he caresses my spine

And rub through my dreads…damn his words are so kind

When he says, "calm down baby, it's ok"…he blows my mind

Holding me, not controlling me…yet sharing his energy…YES, this man was hard to find

Fingers crossed…prayers up…this man..whewww this man has to become mines

If only he was real, my dream would align

~U GenUis~

CHAPTER 2
FAMILY

Dear Mama

Good or bad, right or wrong…Mama I love you

I more so thank you

For keeping me and providing for me too

Although I have pains

That remains

In the depths of my heart, my love for you will NEVER be drained

Nor restrained

There are some things about me that you may never understand

Yet I will always take your hand

To be your strength if ever you can't stand

I will always protect you from the world

I don't care if I'm never your favorite girl

I will always be your smile when you're hurt

I will always pray for you when you feel like dirt

I will always feel your spirit

Even when the pain is whispering and you can barely hear it

My heart will never…EVER close on you

Even when I don't understand the things you do

I love you now and will for an eternity

I just pray that one day you would finally see the best in me

Babygirl

I love you when it's good and more when it's bad

If I was God I'd take away all the stress and pains you ever had

Not knowing what to say to you makes it hard to breathe, this is true

At this point, no matter what, I'd be wrong with every breath…I'm lost right now and I don't know what to do

However, I know that I'd give my life for you

You're my child..I carried you in my womb for 9 months…loving you, nourishing you upon your arrival into this world

Overjoyed because God saw fit to bless me with this beautiful, sinless, yet precious baby girl

The moment I saw you, my heart was stolen by Cupid in his greatest work

Knowing that if anything happened to you I would go berserk

Yes it's been times that you run me crazy…just like right now

But God knows I would be lost without you so we must figure this out somehow

~U GenUis~

My Sons

To my sons,

The young men that I raised alone

I will always protect y'all, right or wrong

No, I couldn't show y'all how to be men from being a man myself

However, I gave y'all the best knowledge I could with absolutely no fatherly help

From racing down the streets

Playing outside in the summer's heat

To praying for strength because mines would get weak

I didn't see the strength that God instilled in me

To raise 3 young men, independently

Now I have 3 grown men and it's much easier to see

And adjust to having grown men to look after me

It's an honor to me to be y'all mother

It sometimes seems I have 3 little brothers

Actually 4 because God gave me another

Another one that I didn't birth but God saw fit for ME to be his mother

Y'all are my joy through my pains

Even though y'all drive me insane

I had to become a masculine woman to raise men

And to be y'all mom, I'll do it again and again

~U Genius~

Safe In His Arms

My oh my…where do I start

Maybe at the part where they ripped out my heart

Made me think my Father didn't love me

Gave me a rare dose of the loneliest reality

Being manipulated by a lie that I thought had truth

Taking my dignity from my youth

Covering marks that has damaged my destiny

Even succumbing the feeling of being surrounded by bad energy

Blinding my eyes so that I could never see

The greatness of the person within me

Closing my ears

So that I couldn't hear

The verbal pain I've encountered over these years

Seeing the man that I once called Daddy

Deceive me

Hurt me

Damage me mentally as well as , physically

God oh God....I know you feel me

Cover me Oh Lord and protect me with your shield

So that one day I can release this burden I've encountered through these years

Maybe one day I can reverse these tears

~U GenUis~

Always My Baby

To my daughter

Whom I raised with no father

You made me change and swallow life as it got harder

Yet you showed me how to love in a more humble way

Gave me your strength when I couldn't make it through my day

Being your mother gave me courage

Your heart, I nourished

Now I'm amazed at the young woman that's flourished

Into being a mother herself

Holding strong…regardless of who left

Being a young lady is hard by itself

Now, you're a mother, if only you know the joy I've felt

Seeig you learning how and when to be strong

Even when you don't feel you belong

Like when every right has a wrong

Because life hits harder than any love song

'm amazed

Sometimes left in a daze

Due to seeing me in a lot of your ways

Wanting to protect you through every phase

Sometimes leaves me outraged

Praying that God keeps you in His arms on your toughest days

I pray for peace and prosperity

Also a husband to be

I pray that God protects you even more than He did for me

May your smile

Glow a ray that stretches over miles

Also may God protect you when you go wild

And always remember that NOT A SOUL WOULD EVER LOVE YOU AS I DO...MY BABYGIRL...MY YOUNGEST CHILD

~U GenUis~

Grandma Boys

Becoming a grandmother was scarier than life, itself

All that I had was the feeling of having grandparents always there to help

For some reason, God saw fit to give me 3 boys again

I pray that I'm here to see y'all become young men

Looking forward to seeing every phase of your lives

The more I look into Y'ALL eyes, the more I strive

Strivig to become better everyday

Aiming to be a better grandma than I was a mother in every way

I will always protect y'all and guide y'all to pray

I will never let go of my love for y'all and there's some things I need to say

Love the Lord, respect your parents and know that I am never too far away

~U GenUis~

CHAPTER 3
BEAREVEMET/INSPIRATIONAL

Missing My Granny

Today makes a whole year

Since you left me, My Dear

I have shedded many tears

Yes, I have no fear

Thank you for instilling in me that God is always right here

Right here with me and never leave my side

You taught me how to feel the Lord, even when I want to hide

Also taught me how to hold my head up and never lose my stride

I miss you so much MAMMO, this is so true

And to think that my life would not physically include you

No one and I mean, no one could ever love me like you

I know in my spirit that their love is not true

Out and so alone out here

I hurt alone, fighting my fears

Even sleep with your picture next to my pillow…yes, I sometimes cry tears

Asking God to allow grace and mercy to take me through these next year

These years without you that I must learn to pray on my own

Yes, I pray…you taught me how to pray strong

But I will forever need you, My Warrior, however you're home

Stay with me in heart, soul and spirit…that's where you belong

It is times that I really need to feel your touch

I cry and I pull on you so much

Never knew there was a pain that hurts as such

Never knew that in life, I will be left so lost

It's like I'm receiving strength, but wasn't prepared for the cost

Becoming more humble, maybe a lot

Now I feel like I'm being run over and left to rot

But you always say it's the damaged fruit that God reached and got?

Your love is unmatched

That's a fact

You showed me how to be a praying woman and to take my life back

While smiling your smile, walking your walk hearing you say UM UM UM, look at her walking like that

~U GenUis~

Unnumbered Years

We started off as friends over 20 years ago

Our friendship weathered storms that only WE really know

We've cried many tears thru these unnumbered years

We've terminated the fake to remain real

We've fallen out but never fought one fight

We can also feel each other's pain without a face in sight

We unselfishly pray for each other's health, finances and don't forget the pain

One day it's yours and the next it's mines…we keep each other sane

Yes, it's been falling outs to where the stubbornness we share pushes us apart

But on this day, I want to tell you that you are the dear to my heart

I know we some gangsters at heart but the love is real

We have real soul ties baby and on this day we will heal!

~U GenUis~

Joy In Pain

It's in these times, we shed tears

Face many fears

Wondering how do we get to tomorrow

Without facing hurt and sorrow

Not realizing that our time is really borrowed

Smile...

Don't drown,

Even if by force

Knowing that God have paved your way through this course

Of hard days

Just don't delay

To give your hurts and sorrows to The Lord as you pray

~U GenUis~

When It's Time

In your time of missing me, know that I will forever be here

I am with you in Spirit, in your soul...I am near

Near not far

I will forever be your twinkling star

So hold on to your strength

Remember God takes you to the highest length

Keep your faith as I have kept mines

I will see you when you get here...when God says it's time

~U GenUis~

Missing My Flo

The days are approaching that makes me remember your pains

From the hurts, sorrows and mental strains

I long for more days with you

Yet God needed you more than I do

So I unselfishly lied when I said to you

"I'll be ok," we both knew that to not be true

Remembering myself looking into your eyes to read your soul

Seeing you begging me not to fold

Holding on to the life stories you've told

You taught me how to stand and to be bold

Bold in Spirit and smile with grace

You were an amazing woman, walked in God's pace

Even to the ones that hurt you…you embraced

Embraced with love and a caring touch

Mammo…FLO! I miss you so much

That my days are sometimes in mental disgust

Like a toilet when it can't flush

Holding all of this pain inside

No, it's not because of my pride

It's because they don't love me Mammo…they lied

They don't talk to me

My pains, they don't see

The hurt the torment of needing your voice and to cope mentally

However I thank you for showing me God to guide me spiritually

Directing me how to embrace my spiritual identity

~U GenUis~

NaKeva Evette

My friend, my sister I will be your strength when you're weakened

Your understanding when you can't think, your legs when you can't stand

My sister, I am willing to be your breath when you can't breathe, just please don't leave

Oh sister, how I love you and can see your smile, also feel your every pain

I know when you're hurting, even thru the smile that don't always shine the same

My sister, blood couldn't bond us but God did because he knew I was the cookie to your cream

Dear sister,I love you from my soul and to know you're down feels like a nightmare, no dream

I lay here in prayer that you can smile at me and make me curse time and time again

Asking God to forgive us of our sins as WE stand in faith for Him to restore your strength, my sister, much more than a friend

~U GenUis~

Recovered Memories

Thinking Cancer took my memory

But it was God all alone, reserving my energy

Blinding me to the pains

The pains, struggles and loneliness of my past, that shit was insane

Sheltering me from those that secretly hates me

All while rebuilding a woman that was broken into pieces that you couldn't see

I was torn…

Yes torn but I had to be reborn

That was the only choice I had in this world where I felt foreign

Remembering when I was a child at Mammo all of the time

She taught me the country living, even how to rod a fishing line

Church every Sunday

If she did nothing else she taught me how to pray

She taught me how to talk to God and don't go astray

Hmmm she even taught me how to flirt because she loved to play

Then being with my aunt was not all so cool

She treated me bad but hell she barely sent her own kids to school

Yet she envied me but uses God as her cover up, but I'm no fool

Her children hunched on me in my sleep

Yea some of my life gets deep

Even when I ran up behind my supposed to be daddy, his nieces did the exact same

Played in our clothes at night, that was a damn shame

Y'all wonder why when I'm mad, I see fire flames

All while when the day ends, I'm always the blame

Even my sister, she loved to see me down

Always tried to make me look like a clown

She talked about everything that differed from them…anything to make me cry or frown

My feet were big and so was my forehead

Even my lips was big, at least that's what she said

Told me all of my life that we don't have the same dad

Then when his mama died, the cousin said the same thing, yea just sad

After I took care of her, even while she was dying

I never knew she would look me in my face and still be lying

But see my Grandpa and Uncle saw the best in me

They loved me beyond what the eyes could see

Their heart was filled with great generosity

I'm not sure who they were to others, but they was everything to me

My protection and my peace

Nevertheless my mama loved me so

However I'm not sure if she sees my pain, you know

Maybe she just can't say the words that's needed to apologize

But see I love her so much and that's no disguise

So I refuse to test what reality shows

I'd rather just not know

Because I don't want to lose her

To no form of sickness or mental detour

All because I just had to selfishly know if that man is not my daddy for sure

~U GenUis~

Grace

The strength within the wings

Makes beautiful of the painful things

Giving understanding of God's being

Acknowledging the beauty in transitioning

Thanking God for Spiritual understanding

Also for strength of loved ones, those left behind

Brighten their smiles, at the times that joy is hard to find

Clear their cloudy days

With joyous sun rays

Give strength to their Spirit with every kneel to pray

Surround them with a love to push harder everyday

Knowing that no matter what, God's love is here to stay

Some days may seem harder than others..THAT'S WHEN YOU STAND

Knowing that our loved ones are ok…they're in God's hands

~U GenUis~

Be of Joy

If Jingle bellls

Could cast a spell

We shall all receive a love that only emotions could tell

Only emotions can express the truth of love

Which is why the holidays makes us miss the loved ones above

Also remember to always have your cheer

Because there will soon be coming a New Year

Where you can release all of the past and present fears

So go ahead and cry out your last tears

Because see now, we are smiling like we have new veneers

Brightly …yet planted securely to the ground

Owning the more relaxed, humble versio of the person that's been found

Being appreciative of the haves and the have nots

Being the coolest breeze when the weather is beyond hotter than hot

Or imagine being the most wanted yacht

Feeling the waves…peace that if only water could tell

Silver bells…

Dear Silver Bells

Please just cast us a joyous spell

~U GenUis~

Love of God

Loving you from a distance

Just don't make common sense

When love used to be our biggest defense

It's now a thing that's of past tense

Truth always stands…while the fake diminishes

Sometimes putting a halt on your finishing

But wait…hold up…don't fail the test

Don't miss what might be for your best

What's real…what's true

It's that only God know who is and who is not really meant for you

This is what the good armor of God will do

His love and protection will see you through

Through life in ways that you never knew

Feeling joy that you've never felt

Realizing that the love of God increases your wealth

Making better of your health

Raising you up from your lowest depths

All because of Jesus wept

And those promises that He promised us, have been kept.

~U GenUis~

Chapter 4

Self-Love

CONFIDENCE

Some call it an ego but I say confidence

Just like some of y'all say, " I'm stressed out!"…but I keep it at a little tense

Understand that what's for me just may not be for you

My blessings are mines, but see God…He got you too

However, don't miss your landing, watching my flight

Because on my journey, I'm the only competitor in sight

Not saying I sit higher than the next human being

I just refuse to watch your ship's movements and let mines sink in

I refuse to be anyone other than me…like it or not, I'm loving on me

I'm loving on these glowing eyes

No matter how many tears they've cried

I'm even loving the thickness and cellulite in my thighs

I'm really loving on that heart that's humbled…in disguise

I learned to love me years ago

Now I'm in love with a woman in me that I refuse to let go

Realizing it's ok to smile and be emotionally free

It's ok just genuinely be me

Allowing my energy

To vibe vibrantly

Thanking God because I was designed just perfectly

Rare Reality

Is there really something wrong with desiring true love and affection that's unseen

Searching for the love you've yearned for can sometimes leave a person mean

Meaning to smile but can't help but frown

Because of all the trash you've gone through and still no one that's true has stuck around

Leaving the heart broken…never fulfilled

Because of the love…the security that's supposed to heal

Has been stereotyped…nothing's real

Leaving you to build a shield

A shield to protect

Not neglect

The fact that what was once broken had given me a different effect

Closing my eyes

Not to die

But to realizing the fact that I am the prize

~U GenUis~

SELF-LOVE

I search for a love that's not given, only received

Retrieved

Yet believed

To one day find me

Not talking just in a relationship where sex is involved

I'm talking about family...building bonds without selfishness, making unity evolve

Love...love that hurts because you don't want to let go

Of family or any type of relationship...making you feel low

Imagine needing a family and no one is there

Then boom...love finds you, now you're breathing clearer air

Love, why do we search so hard for a feeling that we don't understand

Often used in the place of lust from every woman and man

Why just why can't love really be true

However family would even lust, because in their heart, some just don't love you

Love don't see me down

And clearly frown

Or try to use me as a clown

Nor watch me drown

When they can help revive me, you know, don't just hang around

Smiling and knowing you despise me is wild

Better yet...love don't hurt, not on earth...that saying is foul

It's seems like love and hate have a change in their styles

Love has become the most envious emotions

It's like jumping into the wave with no safety, nor precautions

Only to have to realize that you can't soar in that ocean

The tides are too high and the waves are too open

Realizing that's not your type of motion

Love...yes love can also be so real

Even if it's strictly SELF love because that's the first love you should feel

That's the love that heals

See true love often seems surreal

Making some halt at the sight of happiness

Due to always being in distress

Yet, if you hold on and just past this one test

The test of love, it's then that you win

Win back what yours from the beginning

True love that comes from one's self...self-love is very needed

-U GenUis~

Graceful Love

It's often that we dont know where we're going because we haven't acknowledged where we've been

We don't hold on to what we learned and the true value of family and friends

We tend to lose sight of what's real and start following internet trends

We forget that every day won't be all smiles and joy

We start to treat genuine hearts like a refurbished toy

We even see love as an instant pain relief decoy

Not realizing that pain destroy

Your ability to release your spiritual joy

You have to watch your pace

Hold on to your Faith

To protect your happy place

We have to hold on to the good times and have away with those that hurts

Sometimes we have to see the invisible hazards

All signs are not visible to be read

You have to listen for God's voice instead

With the discipline to be lead

And still be a leader on your journey ahead

Know when to hold and when to fold

Understand that even when the weather is hot, it'll one day get cold

But with God as the meteorologist, may my scolds

Be turned into blessed pots of gold

~U GenUis~

Bet On Me Baby

Try being something that you never had

Yet receiving all types of disrespectful backlash

Still working on letting go and making better of my past

Nevertheless you can bet your life that I won't finish last

Revamping the better version of me

Although the visual is all that you all can see

Only because you don't see internally

The strength and courage that lies dominantly

Dominantly within

What you see as just skin

Yes, I have faults…I can't pretend

Pretend like it was always good

Growing up in the hoods

Which is why my strength can sometimes be misunderstood

However…strength also comes with humbleness

Letting go of certain distress

Cleaning the cluttering mess

Giving nothing less

Than my very best

Taking back the good ole days

When life was beautiful and the kids could go outside play

Making life enjoyable for me

See…my vision is sometimes too big to see

Too deep for some that can't feel internally

The anointing on me, Spiritually

However…Try feeling my energy

That's why I say…" Bet On Me Baby" and let's defeat the diversity

~U GenUis~

SELF- DETERMINATION

As people, we can be some ungrateful creatures

Life alone is the biggest blessing that you can secure

We tend to look at what we lost that broke us, which breaks you again

Then you're blinded to the blessings that you're about to gain

Sometimes, we have to make use of the rain

Never let it drain

Your ability to utilize your brain

While this next sentence may make you frown

But you are the only one who can hold you down

We look at no car as though we can't get around

When most of us have feet...just put them on the ground

Place one foot in front of the other and start your stride

That's the problem now... some of us have too much pride

We are too prideful as though our lives had no struggle

We fail to tell the people how we had decisions to juggle

Some ended good and some ended bad

But you woke up to life again...the biggest blessing you've ever had

Especially those of us who have the ability to feel and think on our own

We complain about our lives instead of realizing we are grown

Understanding that no one owes us nothing, we are overly blessed

So stop looking for the world to have the answer key to your test

Sometimes, we need self humiliation

To redirect our mental inspiration

Know that we are in control of us, so be mindful of your intended destination

Nevertheless, you will encounter great frustration

But anything worth achieving takes greater determination.

~U GenUis~

Reminiscing

Reading my words and looking back on my past

Wondering why no one could last

Thinking I was too hard to maybe deal with

Not realizing that they were just too easy to quit

Realizing that there was simply nothing wrong with me

Just simply being vulnerable and desiring loyalty

There is absolutely nothing wrong with me

Wanting to show my femininity

The only real problem was that I did not love me wholeheartedly

I was looking for a mate to see the best of my abilities

Thinking there was something wrong with me

Not seeing the weakness in the masculinity of the men I attracted back there

I had to change some things in me, from within

To attract better mentally stimulated men

Like men that know it's ok to have emotions, love on me baby

If you're hurt, you can cry…work hard and don't be lazy

Allow me to be humble and just be a lady

See I've grown with standards, I'm from the 80s

This tough girl shit is for the crazy

I want to need my man to make my day

With sweet nothings and expressive foreplay

Let me desire you everyday

With dreams of me catching the very next bouquet

~U GenUis~

Made in the USA
Columbia, SC
09 February 2025

53093837R00043